Cooking with Love Care and Fun

by

Rotarian Saumen Ray

Edited and Designed by Rotarian Gill de Warren

Cooking with Love, Care and Fun
by Rotarian Saumen Ray

First published in Great Britian and India 2021 © Saumen Ray
Designed and Edited by Gill de Warren
Kitchen Garden Photography: © Srijit De
Still life photography: © Gill de Warren, Shyamali De, Saumen Ray, Carole Love, Suchira Ray, Jenny Ashton of Silver Apples Photography.

ISBN: 978-1-8384250-0-5
Produced by KARCO'S OF CALCUTTA
Printed in Italy by PIXARTPRINTING

With acknowledgement to the
Directors and Members of
The Rotary Club of Calcutta
RI District 3291

Acknowledgments

I gratefully acknowledge my domestic and international Rotarian friends who found my un-eatable food delicious on Rotary project site visits; chefs of Karco Restaurant (one of the oldest running restaurant in Kolkata, India) with good traditional recipes; a ten year-old boy cooking Chinese momo for his sick mother; my own mother as his 'granny', complementing the boy's dish with coriander chutney; many friends and family members who contributed with recipes; managers of my farmhouse in Kolkata who produced and photographed the kitchen garden fresh vegetables; the participants of my cooking 'Master Classes' in England; my English Editor who diligently complied this unorthodox publication; my life long motivator, Arun Kumar Debath of Harrow, London, a great author; and, most importantly, my 2 year-old grandson who enjoys my fun and food!

If you don't believe it you read it ....

From Chinese Momo to Bengali Coriander Chutney

Youngest Cook to Granny Chef

t De age 10

My Mother age 93

...A Magic Mix of Love

Momo - 16 PIECES

1. Mix 200 gm of cooked and sliced chicken with cabbage, carrot, capsicum, potato and onions (thinly sliced and half fried), in oil with1 tsp of salt, 2 stems of coriander leaves and 4 tsp of soya/black sauce.
2. Make flour into dough with 2 cups of flour and 1/2 cup of water (4:1) and roll it like a thin wrap. Then shape and cut into 12 circular flat pieces.
3. Pour the chicken or vegetarian mix inside each wrap and seal them tightly with the dough in form of a momo, as shown here.
4. Pour water in steamer and boil, brush the divider (with holes) with oil. Place the momos on the top of the divider and cover the steamer. Steam for 20 minutes.
5. Serve with black pepper, chat massala powder, salt and Coriander Chutney

Coriander Chutney

10 stems of coriander leaves,
2 tsp of garlic,
2 tsp of paste or chopped ginger,
3 green chilies with a touch of salt to be put in a mixer without water.

Grind for 5 minutes

Serve as a starter

Simple World Recipes with stories to remember...

Dedicated to my late uncle
Sib Kumar Roy

This is not a book, but a biography of thrilling cooking experience that I have shared with many friends experimenting on how to reach one's heart through food.

I came to England in 1973 to join the second batch of students for a Computer Science (Hons) degree course in London, U.K.

During my journey from London Heathrow Airport to Acton Town on the red bus, number 207, my late uncle Sib Kumar Roy advised me that I should first become a master of ICS, which was then known to be the Indian Civil Service (ICS). What he actually meant was Indian Cooking Service!

The joke then became a reality when I learned cooking during my student life. I later became a British Civil Servant, followed by being a Partner/Director in PwC Management Consultancy in London and India, and owner of one of oldest restaurants in Kolkata - Karco.

Hence, I dedicate this publication to my late uncle Sib Kumar Roy, whose beer I drank, shoes I polished, stories I shared, and dreams I fulfilled, one at least - the Indian Cooking Service!

The vegetables used in the recipes are home-grown in the kitchen garden of my farmhouse near Kolkata, named after Uncle Sib, called 'Shibalaya'.

Contents

Preface

Build immunity with Herbs and Spices

Breaking the Ice with Spice

Comfort dish for Mother and Child

Vegetarian

Vegan

Non Vegetarian

Fun Cooking Stories

Sweet Dish Finish

Are you still hungry?

Bed Time Noodles for Tired Mother

Preface

A little known fact… in the latter half of the 20th Century the Rotary Club of Calcutta introduced brocolli to India, grown in its own centre at Begumpur in the outskirts of Kolkata, West Bengal. The first customer for brocolli was the Grand Hotel of Calcutta.

Since then, this book, is the first ever publication on cookery by a Rotarian from the same Rotary Club, in recorded history. Proceeds from this book will be contributed to The Rotary Foundation to fund children's projects around the world - at home and at school, such as: pure water, equipment and literacy aids in schools; prevention of childhood blindness; water and sanitation in remote villages; and the empowerment of women and girls in education.

Cooking is not a task, it's a pleasure. Health awareness has become more prevalent. Food habits change but we all feel hungry in the same way as Adam and Eve did. Here is an attempt to create a balanced combination of basic dieting needs with available ingredients in order to prepare our body and mind to cope with the stress and strain of everyday life. I find cooking releases such stress, leaving me relaxed and ready to enjoy my food.

Like any medicine, herbs and spices are to be given in right doses. The recipes and quantities of ingredients set out here are not prescriptive, but suggestive. Please note, that one has to avoid any spice or ingredient which may cause an allergic reaction. Please consult your physician if you are in any doubt.

A thirst for food brings saliva to the mouth, which helps us digest. When we watch food being cooked and see the ingredients become food, an instinct arises which increases our appetite. We naturally want to eat when we see and smell. This is particularly useful when children won't eat. Have them watch you cook, and talk through what you are doing. When they get older invite them to help. Make it fun!

Here are some recipes that can be cooked on a range of energy sources including wood, charcoal and microwave oven. I have also included a comfort dish for mother and child to eat and enjoy together.

Preparing food for friends in unusual places can be challenging, such as the time I fed a whole village of 160 people to celebrate my grandmother's 100th birthday with only a clay oven available; the time I escorted two young boy cyclists up the mountains to Darjeeling and fed them with a locally bought rice cooker; and cooking for 10 people for a week at the Hamburg Rotary Convention in 2019, with just a single microwave!

The recipes are influenced from China across to the UK, via India, and I have featured a range of Vegetarian and Vegan recipes, along with a range of Non-vegetarian using lamb, chicken, liver and fish. Also, as a special sweet treat, you will find deserts from India and Africa.

Then, at the end of a long day and you are still hungry, bed time noodles are a quick, nutritious and welcome meal.

Every Taste is Different

Cooking for love, care and fun works equally for restaurants when we keep the Lord Ganesh happy.

Bajrangbali

Hanuman, a monkey god in Hindu Mythology of wisdom, strength, courage, devotion and self discipline. He protects houses against any evil effects. We worship him.

A Hanuman visitor is very rare these days but he comes and spends hours on our balcony eating our food and drinking water from a bucket, near the clay oven. He loves mangoes and bananas.

Thus, the real life God protects us, and our fruits and vegetables, from which this book is compiled.

Build Immunity with Herbs and Spices?

One fine morning we woke up in our college hostel dormitory and my friend said he wanted to open an Indian Restaurant in London. I was taken aback. The concept of an Indian Restaurant those days was rich and greasy food. I proposed to open up a medicine shop next to his restaurant to serve people suffering from stomach upsets after eating in his restaurant. He declined.

Things have changed since then, and people are appreciating the therapeutic values of herbs and spices used in moderation to build better immunity. For example, it's believed that people in the East have a stronger immunity system against viruses such as COVID 19. Spices are no longer a threat but a comfort factor for health. Only consistent usage of these herbs and spices can generate benefits.

Some examples of known therapeutic values of selected herbs and spices are given below:

Green Chili

Can help prevent cancer, low in calories, rich in Vitamins including C, strengthens heart arteries / can help prevent heart attacks. It can control blood sugar, boost bone density, and boost digestion. It is anti-bacterial, anti-oxidant, anti-ulcer, Chili also helps to keep eyes healthy and strengthens the immune system.

Dry Chili, Chili Flakes, Chili Powder

Chili has preventive properties for many ailments such as different types of cancer, rheumatism, stiff joints, bronchitis and chest colds, coughs, headache, arthritis, and heart arrhythmias.

Turmeric/ Haldi
Anti-inflammatory, good for skin, relieves aches and pains, works as a preservative, and helps the digestion.

Cumin (Jeera)
Contains anti-oxidents, helps treat diarrhea, and helps control blood sugar, fights bacteria and parasites. It is anti-inflammatory and helps lower cholesterol.

Garam Massala
Boosts digestion and metabolism, helps fight bloating and flatulence. Removes bad breath.

Garlic (Rasun)
Good for developing immunity, strengthens heart, works as a thinner and purifier of blood, combats common colds and flu when mixed with banana, reduces blood pressure, and aids in the reduction of cholesterol.

Dhania/ Coriander Powder
Reduces skin inflammation, controls blood pressure and diabetes, aids digestion, aids the treatment of osteroporosis.

Coriander (Cilantro) Leaves (Dhania Pata)
Provides magnesium, helps remove toxins from the body, and adds phosphorous. Helps promote liver function, reduce uric acid, and aid bowel movement. Rich in vitamin C and protein, good for the digestive system, good for urine flow, and can help prevent lung and cavity cancers, Also helps cure mouth ulcers, prevent eye diseases, and is good for those who are diabetic.

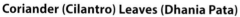

Ginger (Ada)
Helps better blood circulation, digestion, and prevents nausea.

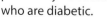

Panch Phoron
Health benefits of panch phoron (made up of five spices) includes weight control, healthy digestion, and has anti-ageing properties.

Black Pepper
Helps reduces blood sugar, improve cholesterol levels, brain and gut health.

Hot Curry Powder
Used in Ayurvedic medicine to help treat inflammation, pain and rheumatoid arthritis.

Lemon
Provides Vitamin C, and helps prevent kidney stones. Used to quell the heat of spices.

Cinamon Sticks (Dal Chini)
Aids sleep, digestion, and is anti-diabetic.

Biryani Mix Spice
Provides authentic taste and aroma for an ultimate food experience. Normally, it includes cumin, bay leaves, cardamom, cinnamon, cloves, red chili, sugar, turmeric, coriander, and oil.

Cloves (Lobongo)
A sweet and aromatic spice which can prevent stomach ulcers. Supports liver health and helps stabilize blood sugar levels 2 and 3.

Bay Leaves
Provides Vitamins A and C, potassium,
calcium, and magnessium.
Helps relieve migrane.
Helps breakdown of protein,
digest food faster,
and reduce indigestion.

Posto (Poppy Seed)
Promotes digestion, boosts skin and hair health, and treats headaches, coughs, and asthma. Helps sleeping at night, and cools the body during heat waves.

Ghee
Ghee is full of omega-3 fatty acids, which are 'good fats', essential for improving the brain and heart health. It also provides energy to the body. So, overall, we can say that ghee is quite nutritious and healthy.

Sultanas (Kismis)
Have high levels of antioxidant activities to protect the body against 'free radicals', cell damage, clogging of arteries and some forms of cancer.

Mint
Aids digestion, keeps mucus at bay, relieves headaches, sooths digestion, has antiviral and antibacterial properties that can ease mild flu and colds.

Mustard (Sorse)
Helps prevent cancer, alleviate asthma, lower cholesterol, relieve muscle spasms and repertory disorders, ease body aches, and aid metabolism.

Cardamom (Elaichi)
Anti-oxidant, reduces water in body, and is anti- inflammatory.

Measuring Ingredients with Spoons
In India, we measure ingredients with teaspoons and tablespoons. The later being complimentary to the fork on the table. In the US, cooking measurements are by the 'cup'. Whereas, in India and UK, a cup is for drinking tea! In the UK a tablespoon is used for serving food and a dessert spoon is laid on the table for eating sweet or dessert. We, therefore, came to the conclusion that the recipes in this book are best measured in semi-heaped teaspoons (tsp). Not flat, except for liquids! That's why eveything is directed in a standard teaspoon(tsp) and may appear, at times, excessive!

Breaking Ice with Spice

A main dish, mainly for children and those feeling sensitive. Very easy and quick to cook with a saucepan.

Pour 4 tsp of cooking oil to make the pan greasy enough to not get dried up at the bottom during cooking.

Add 100 gm of rice, 100 gm of red lentil or yellow (moong) dal, 2 whole tomatoes sliced, 2 peeled potatoes cut in to medium pieces, 2 stems of spring onion cut into medium pieces, 50 gm of green peas, 50 gm of spinach, 1 large skinned carrot cut into small circular pieces, into the saucepan. Add half a litre of hot water.

Fry 2 dry whole chilies in a separate frying pan with 5-6 tsp of cooking oil for 2 minutes, then mix with other ingredients in the sauce pan. Add salt and pepper, to taste.

Cook for 15 mins until the rice and lentils/dal are cooked well. Adjust the quantity of water as necessary to suit your choice.

Add chopped spinach 5 minutes before the end and serve with butter or ghee, and chutney.

Comfort Dish for Mother & Child

Unorthodox Scrambled Egg

A young man travels 20 miles from Ealing to Enfield for work everyday in his old banger car with so many uncertainties on the road. He needs enough strength spending minimum time in the kitchen in his bedsit. Breakfast includes cereal, milk, scrambled egg and toast. He describes here his imaginative recipe for scrambled egg:

Ingredients - SERVES 1

Two eggs
1 onion
1 tsp chili powder
6 tsp milk
4 tsp grated cheese
any cooked vegetable left over from last night, or letttuce
6 tsp cooking oil
Half tsp salt

Direction

While having his first cup of tea or milk with cereal, he chops the onion into small pieces and left over veg or lettuce, if any.

He breaks the eggs into a bowl and mixes with chili powder, grated cheese, onion and milk, and salt. Stirs it well with a fork.

He then pours oil into a frying pan and, when oil is medium hot, he empties the egg mix from the bowl.

He continues to stir well with a fork. The toast is then ready for him.

The scrambled egg will take the appearance and form of sliced white cabbage. It is now ready to eat to make him last the day.

SERVE WITH TOAST
AND/OR BAKED BEANS

Aji Bhaji Street Food
Onion Pakora *(20 pieces)*

Ingredients - SERVES 4

6 medium size white onions
5 stems coriander leaves
2 red chilies
1 green chili
250 gm gram flour
1 tsp salt
250 ml cooking oil
1 cup cold water

Direction

Slice the onions and cut these into small pieces. Empty into a large bowl containing the gram flour. Add salt and one cup water at room temperature. Stir with a fork and, if necessary, use a mixer. Make it into a paste. Add coriander leaves, chopped red and green chilies. Mix them well. Ensure that the density is right enough for frying, like paste, but it shouldn't be too hard, nor liquid. Add water or gram flour as necessary.

Pour cooking oil into a frying pan approx half inch deep. Make the oil very hot. Wear protective gloves and pick up a large spoon of the mix and slowly drop it in the hot oil. It may take on a round shape between 1-2 inches in diameter. Pour as many of these as possible in the frying pan, but keep separate. Lower the temperature of the hob. Fry both sides until the colour turns to light brown . Make sure that the frying is complete and the ingredients inside are cooked. Strain pakoras out of the frying pan and dry on a kitchen towel or wire rack.

Note: You can mix mash or boiled potatoes with the onions too, and prepare Aloo-Piyanj Pakora.

SERVE WITH TEA, SOFT DRINKS, AND CHUTNEY

Health Warning!
Too many of these pakoras eaten in a short period of time may fill you up! Therefore spread them over a period - when watching a football match or a TV serial, prior to lunch or dinner!

French Toast

Ingredients - SERVES 4

Slices of brown or white
bread with crusty edges
2 eggs
Quarter of an onion
1 green chili cut into small
pieces
Quarter of tsp chili powder
1 coriander stem
Quarter tsp salt
1 stem spring onion
2 tomatoes
8 tsp cooking oil

Direction

Break the eggs in a bowl and mix with chopped onion, chili powder, green chili, salt, and sliced coriander leaves. Mix together thoroughly.

Cut the bread into halves. Dip the pieces in the bowl with egg mix. Soak for a few minutes.

Warm up the oil in frying pan and when the oil is hot carefully drop in each piece of soaked bread - one at a time. Fry both sides until the colour turns to light brown. The heat should be a medium heat.

Wait for the breads to become crispy and lay on a kitchen towel.

SERVE WITH TOMATO KETCHUP OR CHUTNEY, TEA/COFFEE, AS SNACKS.

You may wish to serve French Toast for supper with slices of spring onion, red chili, cucumber and roast or sun dried tomatoes.

Dimer Danla
(Egg Curry)

Ingredients - SERVES 4

For every four eggs:
100gm potatoes
Half a capsicum
1 sliced red onion
2 cinnamon sticks
4 bay leaves,
2 tsp garam massala
4 tsp turmeric powder
1 tsp chili powder
2 tomatoes
Tomato ketchup or puree
Hot chili sauce
1 tsp salt
Half tsp white sugar
Slices of lemon
Cooking oil
Red wine (optional)

Direction

Boil the eggs for 6-8 minutes and remove shells. Peel potatoes, cut into approx 3⁄4 inch size chunks and cook for 5 minutes - until half-boiled.

Slice the red onion and fry in light oil until semi brown. Add cinnamon sticks, bay leaves and eggs. Fry for 2 minutes.

Add turmeric, chili powder and garam masala, then fry together adding salt and sugar. Add tomatoes and potatoes, and continue to fry . If necessary, add tomato ketchup and chili sauce (to your taste), during frying.

Add a few tablespoons of red wine if you wish. In absence of red wine, you may add a few slices of lemon - during fryng.

Add hot water and boil to simmer until the potatoes are cooked. Choose water level to your preference for gravy or dry.

SERVE WITH RICE, WRAPS, OR FLAT BREAD

Mixed Race Khinchuri
(main dish)

Ingredients - SERVES 4

100 gm basmati rice
100 gm yellow dal
100 gm red lentil
1 cauliflower
2 Indian radish (Mulo)
100 gm green peas
100 gm potatoes
150 gm white onion
50 gm garlic
10 green chilies
6 tsp turmeric powder
2 tsp chili powder
4 tsp garam masala
6 bay leaves
100g butter
4 tsp sugar
2 tsp salt
4 dry chilies
Hot water

SERVE WITH ONION PAKORAS,
NAKED AUBERGINE, ALOO PAKORAS,
CALIFLOWER FRITTER, CHUTNEY,
OMLETTE OR ANY OTHER SIDE DISH

Direction

Skin the potatos and cut into pieces of approx 1 inch in size. Cut the cauliflower into pieces of 2 inches in size. Cut the onions into chunks of 4 from a small onion and 8 from a medium size onion. Grate or slice the garlic.

Fry the cauliflower, Indian radish and potatoes with dry chilies for about 10 minutes. Empty these into another container. Fry onion, garlic, lentil and yellow dal in a sauce pan for 5 minutes. Add rice, turmeric, chili power and garam masala. Continue to fry, add salt and sugar.

After 5 minutes pour hot water - about half a litre. There should be enough water covering the ingredients. If necessary add extra water. Boil for 10 minutes and then add the cauliflower, Indian radish and potato mix. Continue to boil. Stir intermittently to ensure the mix doesn't get dry and stick to the bottom of the pan.

Cover the sauce pan and simmer for another 15 minutes until lentil, yellow dal and rice are cooked well. When it's nearly there, add the butter and cover. We want the ingredients to be well cooked, not over cooked.

Aloo Sabji Express

Ingredients - SERVES 4

100 gm potatoes
1 cauliflower
1 Indian radish
100 gm green peas
5 green chilies
5 coriander stems
50 gm green beans
4 tsp turmeric powder
1 tsp chili powder
1 tsp salt
1 tsp white sugar
4 tsp garam masala
2 cinnamon sticks
50 ml cooking oil
Hot water

Direction

Skin the potatoes and cut into pieces of approx 3⁄4 inch. Cut cauliflower into florets of 2 inches long and cut beans and raddish into smaller pieces.

Pour oil into the saucepan and heat. Fry potatoes, beans, green chilies, radish, and cauliflower for 5 minutes.

Add turmeric, chili powder, garam massala, cinnamon sticks, sugar, and coriander leaves, then fry for a further 5 minutes.

During frying, ensure that the mix doesn't stick to the bottom of the pan - keep stiring.

When the cauliflower becomes half-brown, add 50 ml of hot water and cover the vegetables. Add salt and stir. Let it boil for 10 minutes, covered with the lid. Add extra water, if required, to boil the vegetables.

Once the vegetables are cooked through remove the lid, and simmer for 2 minutes, or so, to make a thicker gravy.

SERVE AS A SIDE DISH WITH RICE, WRAP OR FLAT BREAD

Spicy Chickpeas

Ingredients - SERVES 4

200 gm chick peas
100 gm small potatoes
2 white onions
1 red onion
8 tsp tomato puree
6 tsp chana/chat masala powder
4 tsp cumin
4 tsp turmeric
4 tsp garam masala
4 bay leaves
6 dry chilis
4 coriander leaves
1 tsp salt
Half a litre hot water
Lime juice (lemon)

Direction

Soak chickpeas overnight in water. Boil to 75% cooked and strain, keeping the water in which it was boiled.

Peel the potatoes leaving some skin on. Slice white onions and fry in a saucepan for 5 minutes along with dry chili. Add semi-boiled chickpeas and peeled potatoes to the pan.

Add turmeric, cumin, garam masala, bay leaves, and salt. Fry for 5 minutes then add hot water and the water in which the chickpeas were boiled.

Now boil for 10 minutes with lid on until chickpeas and potatoes are fully cooked.

This should be a thick gravy type dish. You may have to add water as necessary. If the mix becomes too thin, boil with the lid open.

Finish by adding lime juice.

SERVE WITH SLICED RED ONION AND SLICES OF GREEN CHILIS, CHANA/CHAT MASALA POWDER - TO GO WITH TEA, COFFEE, OR SOFT DRINKS AS SNACKS

Spanish Spinach
(side dish)

Spinach is probably the most common vegetable across the world, although it started its first usage in Spain. It is also one of healthiest and easiest to cook.

Ingredients - SERVES 4

250 gm spinach leaves
1 aubergine
100 gm potatoes
6 sliced green chilies
2 tsp panch phorong (five spices)
10 -12 tsp cooking oil
2 tsp turmeric powder
1 tsp chili powder
1 tsp salt

Direction

Wash the spinach leaves.

Pour oil into a frying pan and when hot add the panch phorong and fry for one minute.

Add potatoes cut in quarter inch chunks, sliced aubergine and green chilies. Fry for 10 minutes.

Add salt and then empty spinach into the frying pan. Stir and fry for another 5-10 minutes until spinach changes its colour and potatoes are soft.

Include mushrooms as an alternative, or as well as, aubergines.

SERVE TO ACCOMPANY ANY MAIN RICE DISH

Naked Aubergine
Spicy Aubergine

When you return home from work and find there are no vegetables in your fridge except some old aubergines, as orphans. But you require something exotic. This is what you do in those circumstances.

Ingredients - SERVES 2

1 Aubergine
Cooking oil
4 tsp turmeric powder
1 tsp chili powder
4 dry chilies
2 tsp lemon jiuce
Half tsp salt
Coriander leaves
Red wine (optional)
Hot water

Direction

Naked Aubergine

Cut 1 aubergine into slices like a tyre. Sprinkle 4 tsp turmeric powder and salt. Keep for 15 minues. Pour oil into a frying pan and shallow fry until brown.

Spicy Aubergine

Cut 1 aubergine in cubes approx 1 inch in size. Pour oil into a frying pan and fry dry chilies. Add the aubergine pieces and fry with turmeric and chili powder. Fry well with oil. Add lemon juice and stir.

When the colour is brown, add one cup hot water and boil to simmer. Once the gravy becomes thick, turn off the hob and sprinkle four stems of coriander leaves, cut into pieces, and let the dish rest for 10 minutes.

You may add 3 tbsp of red wine during frying if you wish.

SERVE WITH RICE DISH, WRAP, LOOCHI * OR FLAT BREAD

* See Loochi recipe no. B9

Tiger Posto
Poppy Seeds

The district of Birbhum in West Bengal is one of the hottest places. We were there working all day in the villages, doing social work. Exhausted, we finally rested on camp beds in front of our forest bungalow. Some of us were dehydrated - some were drinking beer, some drinking salt and lemon water. We also wanted something for dinner that was soothing. The local Adibashi women made rice, dal and tiger posto for us, which made us relax and sleep peacefully that night, ready for the next day. Here is how they made tiger posto - poppy seeds.

Ingredients - SERVES 4

250 gm of potatoes
6 dry chilies
6 green chilies
100 gm posto (poppy seeds)
2 spring onion stems
1 tsp chili powder
1 tsp salt
50 ml cooking oil or mustard oil (if available)
1 tsp turmeric powder
2 cups hot water

Direction

Soak posto and green chilies overnight in water. Use a mixer/grinder to paste posto and chilies together, adding only a few drops of water.

Peel potatoes and cut them into small sizes of approx half an inch. Pour oil in frying pan and fry the potatoes for 5 minutes. Then add the pasted posto, turmeric powder, and salt. Fry for two minutes, then add hot water.

Bring to boil and simmer for 10 -15 minutes, adding chopped spring onions during the boiling.

SERVE WITH RICE WRAP, OR FLAT BREAD

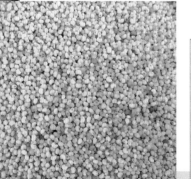

Aloo Pakora Street Food
(Potato) 20 pieces

Sometimes it's difficult to arrange food for guests who are Vegan. A friend arrived one evening at dinner without the host knowing that they were vegan, where the others were clearly non-vegetarian. At that time of night, the host had run out of ideas until his wife told him that Aloo Pakora would go nice with Vegetable Pilau and lentils. The kitchen got busy again. What was made for the vegan guest became the favorite for all, as a pre-dinner snack. This is how it was made:

Ingredients - SERVES 5-6

Six medium size potatoes
Half a stem coriander leaves
2 red chilies
250 gm gram flour
1 tsp salt
250 ml cooking oil
2 cups cold water

Direction

Slice the potatoes into the shape of slim line finger chips . Empty into a large bowl containing the gram flour. Add salt and one of cup water at room temperature. Stir with a fork - if necessary, use a mixer. Make it into a paste. Add coriander leaves and chopped red chilies. Ensure that the density is right for frying - like paste - not too hard, nor is it liquid. Add water or gram flour, as necessary.

Make your frying pan hot. Pour cooking oil into the pan and make the oil very hot. Wear protective gloves and pick up a large spoon of the mix and slowly drop it in the hot oil. It may take on a round shape, between 1-2 inches in diameter. Pour as many of these as possible into the frying pan. Lower the temperature of the hob. Fry both sides until the colour turns to light brown. Make sure that the frying is complete and test the inside is cooked. Strain pakoras and dry on a clean kitchen towel or wire rack.

SERVE WITH TEA, DRINKS AND CHUTNEY
ALSO WITH ANY MAIN DISH OR FLAT BREAD

Cauliflower Florentine

Cauliflower, if not cooked well, gives out an odor that some people might not like. We had a funny little boy at home who didn't like cauliflower. Hence this innovative recipe was developed:

Ingredients - SERVES 4

1 Cauliflower
1 capsicum
100 gm potatoes
1 courgette
2 tomatoes
4 tsp turmeric
1 tsp chili powder
4 tsp garam masala
4 cardamom pods
8-10 cloves
2 cinnamon sticks
6 coriander stems
1 tsp salt
1 tsp sugar
50 ml cooking oil
250 ml hot water
White wine (optional)

Direction

Cut the cauliflower into small florets, chop courgette and potatoes into small pieces, cut aubergine into slices, chop tomatoes, and slice the capsicum.

Pour a little oil in a pan and fry the cauliflower, potatoes and capsicum along with cinnamon sticks and cloves, for 5 minutes. Add turmeric, chili powder, sugar, salt, and cardamom pods, and fry together for another 5 minutes . Add chopped tomatoes, half tsp salt and about half a cup of white wine (optional). Continue to fry. When the cauliflower changes its colour to light brown, add hot water and simmer with the lid on until vegetables are cooked. If you have tomato puree or Tabasco sauce sprinkle lightly, for extra heat and flavour.

Control the quantity of water depending on your prefered thickness of the gravy. Sprinkle cut coriander leaves and simmer with lid on for 15 minutes.

SERVE WITH RICE DISH, WRAP, OR FLAT BREAD

Parwal Shanks
(Potol)

Parwal is mini version of courgettes, available in Indian and Pakistani shops and markets. If you wish to treat somebody who will go back and remember the new dish, you may decide to cook it as follows:

Ingredients - SERVES 4

500 gm parwal (approx 12-14 pieces)
200 gm potatoes
4 tsp turmeric
2 tsp jeera (cumin) powder
4 tsp garam masala
2 tsp chili powder
2 tsp dhania (coriander) powder
50 ml mustard oil (if not available use vegetable oil)
2 tsp salt
250 ml hot water

Direction

Cut both the end of each parwal and peel potatoes. Sprinkle about half the turmeric powder on parwal and potatoes.

Pour oil into a pan and fry for 5-7 minutes until parwals turn slightly tan.

Then add the garam masala, dhania powder, jeera powder, chilli powder, salt and remaining turmeric powder. Continue to fry for another 5 minutes. You may add extra chili or Tabasco sauce, if you wish.

Add hot water and boil for 10-15 minutes with lid covering the pan. When parwals are cooked, remove the lid and dry up the gravy, by simmering.

SERVE WITH RICE DISH, WRAP, FLAT BREAD, OR LOOCHI

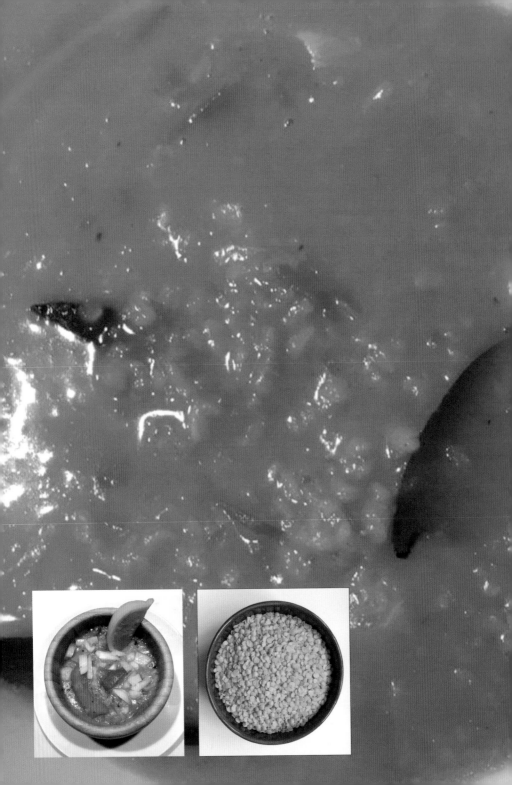

Versatile Lentils

Ingredients - SERVES 4

100 gm of half-broken
red lentils
4 tsp garlic paste
4 tsp ginger paste
2 tsp turmeric powder
1 tsp chili powder,
5 dry chilies
2 cinnamon sticks
4 bay leaves
50 ml cooking oil or butter
4 tsp salt
Half a litre hot water

Direction

Fry dry lentils in a saucepan with hot oil or butter on low heat for 2 minutes.

Add turmeric, ginger paste, garlic paste, chili powder, dry chilies, salt, cinnamon sticks, and bay leaves. Continue to fry and stir for 5 minutes. Add hot water and boil for 15 minutes on medium heat. Cover with lid. Check the density and add hot water, as appropriate. Top with chopped onion and lemon when eaten as soup.

ANY VEGETARIAN, VEGAN OR
NON-VEGETARIAN SIDE DISH

Ghee Bhaat
Butter Rice (main dish)

Ingredients - SERVES 4

200 gm basmati rice
Quarter packet of butter
Half tsp salt
Water.

Direction

Soak the rice in water for an hour, or so. Empty rice into a small saucepan. Pour water to a level when rice is half and water above is half again. For example, if the depth of rice is quarter inch you should add water to make it half inch, in total. Add 1 tsp of white cooking oil and salt. Boil for 6 minutes with lid on, then add butter and let it simmer for another 5 minutes.

Peas Pillaw
(Main Dish)

Pillaw is normally very rich. However, a simpler and quicker version of it is Peas Pillaw goes a long way, and it impresses people

Ingredients - SERVES 4

200 gms basmati rice
Half a packet of butter
200 gm peas (fresh or frozen)
2 carrots
5 cinnamon sticks
20 cardimom pods
20 cloves
4 tsp sugar
1 tsp salt
4 bay leaves
20 cashew nuts
Half cup cooking oil.

Direction

Soak peas, cashews, and rice in water separately overnight.

Half cook the rice in a saucepan and strain. In a separate saucepan, pour in the oil and fry cinamon stick, cardimom pods, and bay leaves, with grated carrots for 3 minutes.

Add the rice, cashews, and cloves and fry for 5 minutes. Add half the butter, sugar and peas, and fry for further 10 minutes.

You may add a little hot water, cover with lid, and let it all simmer on very low heat for 15 minutes.

SERVE WITH RICE DISH, WRAP, FLAT BREAD, OR LOOCHI

Loochi

Ingredients - SERVES 2

100 gm flour
2 tsp sugar
1 tsp salt
1 cup of hot water
100 ml of cooking oil

Direction

Empty flour into a large bowl and add salt, sugar and oil (as prescribed). Make into a dough with hot water. Make 12 separate dough balls. Roll each one into a flat disc shape, say 2-3 inches in diameter. Spread them on kitchen work top or a tray.

Put a frying pan on the hob and pour in 100 ml of cooking oil so that it can be deep fried. Let the oil heat up well. Now drop the dough discs flat on the oil, carefully. After half a minute turn over. It grows with air inside and turns into the shape of a 'Big Mac'! You may turn it over again, if necessary, otherwise strain and place on wire rack or kitchen towel. Fry 12 pieces one by one.

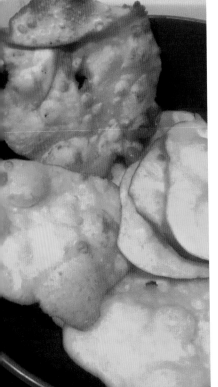

Golden Triangle

Aubergine Shank *(Main)*

Ingredients - SERVES 2

1 whole aubergine
4 tsp turmeric powder
1 tsp salt
50 ml cooking oil

Direction

Slice aubergine longitudinally making an aubergine into 4 or 8 slices - like shanks. Add turmeric and salt, and deep fry in pan with oil, turning to all sides.

When the colour becomes dark, it's ready. Strain out the aubergines from the pan on to kitchen paper or wire rack.

Aloo Dum

Ingredients - SERVES 2

250 gm small potatoes
4 medium size tomatoes
2 cinnamon sticks
4 tsp garam masala powder
4 bay leaves
4 tsp turmeric powder
2 tsp chili powder
1 tsp salt
2 tsp jeera powder (cumin)
1 capsicum
6 green chilies

Direction

Cut potatoes into small pieces, chop tomatoes, and slice capsicum. Put the used oil from Loochi or some fresh oil into a saucepan. Empty potatoes, tomatoes and capsicum into the pan and fry for 5 minutes. Add cinnamon sticks and bay leaves together. Also add turmeric powder, garam masala, salt, and chili powder. Fry for further 5 minutes, than add slices of green chili. Stir for a few minutes .
Pour boiling water and boil, cook until you get a thick gravy.

SERVE WITH ANYTHING AND
EVERYTHING AT ANY TIME, ANY DAY

Instant Mango or Apricot Chutney

In the old days, once the hunger is met by dinner, people use to continue to sit and chat about things they would otherwise not talk about. It is the 'chat' about others or other subjects, like an 'any other business' item on a meeting agenda. That gave the name 'CHUTNEY'. The situation is still the same now, I believe. To stimulate discussions, chutney works as a catalyst. Therefore, chutney is a must for chatting, which is perhaps the most important part of a dinner. Here is the recipe for instant chutney (makes 2-3 jars).

Ingredients

1 jar of apricot or mango jam
100 gms sultanas
50 gms sugar
6 tsp turmeric powder
4 dry chilies
4 bay leaves
100 gm water-soaked cashew nuts
2 cinnamon sticks
12 cloves
12 cardamom pods
50 ml cooking oil
1 tsp salt
2 cups hot water

Direction

Soak cashews and sultanas in water overnight.

Pour oil into a frying pan and heat well. Add dry chilies, bay leaves, cinnamon sticks, and cashew nuts. Fry for a couple of minutes then add sugar. Fry and caramelize for a further couple of minutes - this will give it a good colour. Add turmeric powder, cardamom pods and salt, and fry for a further minutes, or so.

Pour the whole jar of jam and sultanas into the sauce pan and fry for 5 minutes. When the mixture thickens add hot water and stir. Cook for 15 minutes adding water depending on the thickness of the cooked material. Once finished empty into a bowl and leave to cool. Decant into sterile jars, seal, and store in a cool place or fridge.

Special Note:
Recipe also works with any jam or even a mix fruit jam. You may use fresh mango, cut into small pieces and boiled for 10 mins before following the above recipe.

Chicken Hurry Curry

Chicken curry cooked in hurry. Why? Here is a story:
We plan things, but things change and give us a new challenge, for example:
We were on a social service project in the remotest part of Birbhum district, in West
Bengal. Eight of us left Kolkata at 8am. We arrived in Birbhum at 2pm, did social
service work until 6pm, then returned to the nearest town - Santiniketan - at 7pm,
that evening. We had to feed eight people, as well as write up notes of our meetings, in
preparation for the next day. We had to cook a meal in a hurry. Unfortunately, the cook
of the house where we were staying had left for the day.

Ingredients - SERVES 8

We carried with us 2 kg of chicken cut into pieces, onions, and potatoes.

We found ginger and garlic paste in the kitchen, along with a pressure cooker, rice grains, turmeric dust etc.

In the garden we found green chilies and coriander.

The boys were tired and didn't feel like working again. We had to cook something quickly to keep their motivation going.

SERVE WITH RICE DISH, WRAP, FLAT BREAD, OR LOOCHI

NOTE:
Double the cooking time if using a regular cooking pan, and test the meat is cooked.

Direction

We put chicken pieces into a bowl mixed with 8 tsp of turmeric powder, 8 tsp garlic and 8 tsp ginger paste, 2 tsp salt, and a tiny bit of yogurt, left over by the caretaker's wife.

We took out the pressure cooker, fried 12 chopped green chilies and 500 gm of sliced onions, then poured over the chicken pieces and potatoes, along with a glass of red wine (optional) and fried everything together. The food was cooked in 20 minutes. In the meantime, the rice was cooked along with peas from the garden. But, when we opened the pressure cooker we found the chicken was still tough. Measures were taken by adding quarter of a green papaya from the garden to soften the chicken...(tip!)

They slept well with the spices cooked in the pressure cooker, mixed with red wine. The next morning they were as fresh as a morning rose, and we started the day.

Chicken and Egg Dilema!

Did you ever think of mixing Chicken with Egg? It might happen at times. In your home it is very rare that you have the perfect situation for everyone. For example, you don't know how many friends your son will bring home past 10pm! On one such occasion a mother was very distressed when she saw her son arriving home unexpectedly with two of his friends, and their girl friends. She had only eight pieces of chicken already cooked in a curry, but how will serve the extra mouths? There is no more chicken left, but plenty of eggs. Her son asked, "What have you cooked for us?" She reluctantly replied, "Chicken or Egg". One of the older boys suddenly said, "You mean Chicken and Eggs!". She replied "Exactly as that".. She jumped on it.

Ingredients - SERVES 6-8

8 pieces ready-cooked chicken as a base
6 eggs
6 pieces of potato
2 tsp turmeric powder
1 tsp chili powder
8 tsp cooking oil
Half tsp salt

Direction

In the kitchen, she half-boiled the eggs, peeled them, and fried with turmeric and chili powder to give a tanned look. She then added the potatoes to the eggs, together with salt, and poured over hot water, to boil for 8 minutes. She mixed the egg preparation with the cooked chicken and cookd for a further 5 minutes. The food was ready.

Her son's friend asked her, "Aunty is this chicken or egg"? She replied, "What comes first, chicken or egg? You are in a dilemma! If you do not know the answer, then just eat it"! The boy said, "Mam, this is a chicken and egg situation, you are more intelligent than my parents!" The food was absorbed tastily – mixing chicken with egg. None of them had tasted this before in their lives, and they loved it.

SERVE WITH RICE DISH, WRAP, FLAT BREAD, OR LOOCHI

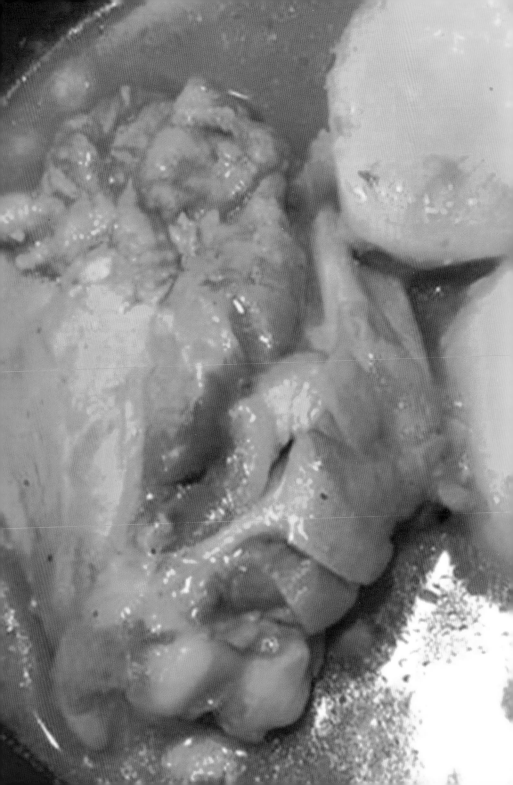

East Meets West Chicken Casserole

Convergence of Indian and British cooking is evident, in many areas. For example Beef Goulash, Chicken Tikka Massala, and Lamb Hotpot are just some of the examples of convergence. Another item of convergence is Chicken Casserole and Indian Chicken Curry. This recipe for 'East Meets West Chicken Casserole' explains it all.

Ingredients - SERVES 4

1 kg of boneless chicken
250 gm potatoes
2 large carrots
1 capsicum
2 large white onions
4 green chilies
4 tsp turmeric powder
1 tsp chili powder
50 gm natural yogurt
1 pkt chicken casserole mix
3 level tsp Tabasco sauce
1 tsp salt
50 ml cooking oil
Half glass red wine (optional)
Half litre hot water

Direction

Peel onions and potatoes and slice. Cut capsicum into 1 inch x half-inch size. Cut green chilies into small pieces. Cut carrots to approx quarter inch thick.

Pour oil in sauce pan and fry onion until brown. Add chicken, turmeric, chili powder, green chilies, natural yogurt, and carrots, and fry for 5 minutes. Add half a glass of red wine if you wish, or juice from half a lemon, and fry for further 5 minutes.

Add capsicum, potatoes, chicken casserole mix, hot water, and salt. Boil to simmer stirring occasionally for 15 minutes with lid on. Add Tabasco sauce during boiling. Add hot water if necessary, to the thickness of the gravy that you prefer.

Let it rest for half an hour before serving.

SERVE WITH RICE DISH, BOILED POTATOES OR VEGETABLES

Valentine Chicken / Lamb (Dopiazza)

The Valentine is meant for only two. The best gift that a well known chef in North India could give to his heart-throb was a specifically designed dish for her, that may not fly like "gone with the wind", but romantic enough in its meaning. Hence he prepared a dish for "Do" meaning two, made only with two main ingredients — meat and onion. The name Dopizza came about. This is, at least, what the chef believed.

Ingredients - SERVES 4

1 kilo boneless chicken/lamb
250 gm small potatoes
250 gm white onions
2 courgettes
250 gm red onions
50 gm garlic
50 gm ginger
6 tsp turmeric powder
1 tsp chili powder
4 tomatoes
4 green chilies
2 dry chilies
50 ml mustard oil or cooking oil
2 tsp garam masala powder
2 tsp salt
1 tsp white sugar
8 -10 tsp natural yogurt
Half litre hot water
Half cup red wine (optional) or
quarter of a lemon

Direction

Cut chicken / lamb into approx one inch size pieces and marinade with natural yogurt, turmeric, and half tsp salt for about 30 minutes.

Fry dry chilies and thinly sliced white onions, with crushed garlic and ginger, for 5 minutes in a deep frying pan. Empty the chicken/lamb into the frying pan together with potatoes and sliced courgettes (like tyres). Fry for 10 minutes adding red wine or lemon juice, chopped tomatoes, and salt.

Add hot water and simmer for 15 minutes for chicken, or 45 minutes for lamb. When halfway through the cooking, add the red onions cut into 8 chunks each. One may add 5-6 tsp of Tabasco sauce towards the end for extra heat and flavour.

Sprinkle over sliced coriander leaves and let it rest for half an hour, with lid closed.

SERVE WITH RICE DISH, FLAT BREAD WRAP OR LOOCHI

Kasa Mangso

The word 'kasa' means close encounter. Mangso, in this case, means lamb, mutton or chicken. Even nowadays, at Dromolamd Castle, Dublin, Ireland, they hold medieval banquets where chicken and meat pieces are eaten with fingers, without knife and fork, or anything else. The concept of 'kasa' came much earlier. In today's context, Mangso mixed well with only spices is Kasa Mangso.

Ingredients - SERVES 4

1 Kg of Mangso (boneless chicken or lamb) cut into pieces of approx 1 inch
250 gm white onions
8 tsp ginger paste
8 tsp garlic paste
4 tsp turmeric powder
2 tsp chili powder
4 tsp garam masala
100 gm natural yogurt
50 gm tomato puree
4 tomatoes
4 green chilies
1 tsp salt
100 ml cooking oil
2 tsp Tabasco or chili sauce
Half litre hot water
Glass red wine (optional)
Green papaya (if you have)
2 tsp Madras hot curry powder could be handy

Direction

Marinade the Mangso in turmeric and yogurt, with half tsp salt, for about 2 hours.

Using a deep pan, fry onions in oil with turmeric and little chili for about 5 minutes. Add Mangso and all species listed here. Fry and stir well for 15 minutes. You may add Madras hot curry powder. This is known as the process - 'kasa'.

Pour in hot water, add half tsp salt, and boil for 45 minutes until the meat is soft. If the meat is still tough, drop a piece of green papaya to speed up the process. Otherwise, just boil for longer period, adding hot water. Control the quantity of water input to suit your taste and the thickness of the gravy.

Add chopped coriander leaves. Let the dish rest for half an hour, with the lid on.

SERVE WITH RICE DISH, FLAT BREAD WRAP OR LOOCHI

Niramish Mangso
Lamb / Mutton

It was the Kali Puja / Dewali / Festival of Lights, and the Goddess Kali is offered a meat dish, which we then all eat after the worship. It is a challenge to cook without garlic or onion. Some changes have been made in the method of cooking and some special ingredients have been added, as follows:

Ingredients - SERVES 4

1 Kg Mangso (Lamb or Mutton) cut into pieces 1 inch
500 gm of small potato
4 dry chilies
2 tsp white sugar
2 tsp salt
5 tsp turmeric powder
2 tsp chili powder
4 tsp garam masala
6 bay leaves
2 cinnamon sticks
1 tsp cloves
3 tsp jeera powder (cumin)
3 tsp dhania powder (coriander)
2 tsp cardamom pods
100 gm natural yogurt
4 tomatoes
4 green chilies
1 tsp whole black pepper
100 ml white oil
6 coriander stems
Half - 3/4 litre of hot water
2 glasses red wine (optional)
A piece of green papaya would be useful if you have some

Direction

Marinade the Mangso in turmeric, jeera, dhania, natural yogurt, and 1 tsp salt for a couple of hours.

In a saucepan fry dry chilies, cinnamon sticks, bay leaves, and sugar for 3 minutes in white oil. Add mangso, cloves, garam massala, cardamom pods, whole black pepper, salt, and sliced green chilies. Fry together with red wine, stirring for about 15 minutes.

Pour on hot water, add salt and boil for 45 minutes, until the meat is soft. If the meat is still tough, drop a piece of papaya to speed up the process. Otherwise just boil for longer period, adding hot water. Control the quantity of water input so that you end up with thick gravy.

Let it rest overnight. Next day, heat it up with chopped coriander leaves, and serve.

SERVE WITH RICE DISH, FLAT BREAD WRAP OR LOOCHI

Mince Korma
Lamb / Mutton / Chicken

Korma is a fascinating name. Once we were passing an Indian Restaurant, the name Korma caught the eye of my daughter. Korma is normally very spicy and suitable only for strong stomachs and occasional consumption. But my daughter insisted that we have it because her friends loved it. Therefore, a hybrid recipe came out of our kitchen which can be eaten as often as you wish - without the need for digestive tablets!

Ingredients - SERVES 4

1 kg minced lamb/ mutton/ chicken
500 gm onions chopped to medium size chunks
500 gm small potatoes (or large potatoes cut to small sizes approx 1 inch)
100 ml cooking oil
50 gm chopped garlic
50 gm grated (or 2 tsp ginger paste)
4 tsp turmeric powder
2 tsp chili powder
4 tsp garam masala powder
2 cinnamon sticks
1 tsp salt
4 tomatoes chopped
1 capsicum sliced
Natural yogurt
100 gm green peas
6 green chilies split into halves along the length
Half litre hot water

Direction

In a large saucepan, fry the onions for 5 minutes. Add cinnamon sticks, garlic, and potatoes, and fry for 2 minutes. Add ginger, garam massala, turmeric, capsicum, green chilies, chili powder, and meat, and fry for 10 minutes, adding tomatoes halfway.

Add half a glass of red wine (or natural yogurt) and salt. Stir for 5 minutes until the meat is semi-dark in colour.

Add hot water and a boil well until meat and potatoes are cooked. Towards the end, add green peas.

Simmer to your taste and density, adding water as necessary.

SERVE WITH RICE DISH, FLAT BREAD WRAP OR LOOCHI, AND CHUTNEY

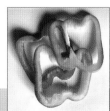

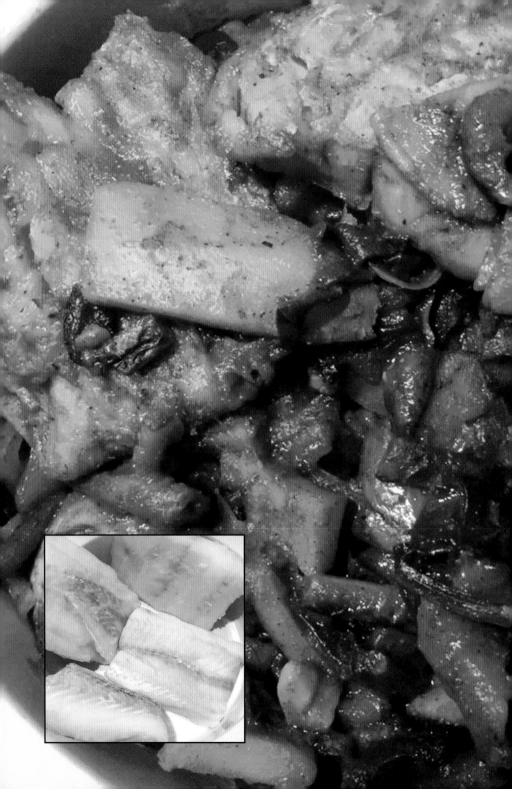

Spicy Cod

Are you tired of eating Cod and Chips? Try something new, now.

Ingredients - SERVES 2

400 - 500 gm cod fillets
6 tsp tumeric powder
I tsp salt
100ml cooking oil
100 gm white onions
50 gm garlic
1 capsicum
2 tomatoes
1 tsp chili powder
200ml hot water

SERVE WITH RICE DISH, FLAT BREAD WRAP OR LOOCHI

Direction

Cut cod fillets into 4 pieces and sprinkle on turmeric powder and salt. Rest for 1 hour.

Pour oil into a frying pan and fry the cod well, both sides. Empty the fish onto a side plate.

Fry sliced onion and grated garlic together with sliced capsicum and sliced tomatoes until the onions become semi-brown. Add chili powder during frying along with hot water and salt, to taste.

Once it starts boiling place the cod pieces on top and simmer for 10 minutes, turning it into a saucy dish.

Spanish covered Cod and Eggs

Direction

Same as Spicy Cod, add 2 boiled eggs and 100gm green beans during frying, then sprinkle thin cut spinach leaves during the last 3 minutes of cooking.

Drunken Sardines

There are times when we feel lazy and not doing anything other than watching the television. Simple recipes that can be used to cook something mouth watering.

Ingredients - SERVES 2

400-500 gm canned sardines
50 gm small onions
50 gm garlic
Aubergine, capsicum and/or courgette
1 tsp curry powder or leaves
1 tsp chili powder
I cinnamon stick
1 tsp salt
6-8 tsp white wine (optional) or juice fron half a lemon
Hot water

SERVE WITH RICE DISH, FLAT BREAD WRAP OR LOOCHI

Direction

Drain two x 200 gms canned sardines from oil. Fry cut onions and cut/grated garlic into a frying pan with sliced aubergine, and/or capsicum, and/or courgetttes. Add the curry powder, chili powder, and cinnamon during frying. If you don't have curry powder add some curry leaves or turmeric powder instead. Add the fish and salt (to taste) and fry for about 10 minutes. Add white wine, if you wish, or juice from half a lemon.

When the colour becomes dark, add one or two cups of hot water and stir to simmer for 5 minutes. Your food is ready.

Tuna Midnight Feast

You want to have a midnight feast which is very light and easy to cook...

Ingredients - SERVES 2

400-500 gm canned tuna
100 gm sliced onion
4 tsp ginger paste
4 tsp garlic paste
4 green chilis
100 ml white oil
4 tsp natural yogurt
Glass white wine (optional)
Two spring onion stems

Direction

Drain canned tuna.
Fry sliced onion with ginger paste, garlic paste, and green chilies for 5 minutes with 100m white oil. Add the the fish and stir. Then add the natural yogurt and a glass of white wine (if you wish). Stir well and fry for 10-15 minutes adding the spring onions cut into pieces.

Floating Trout

A housewife bought two whole Rainbow Trout. Her son and daughter do not like the head or tail, so she asked the fishmonger to make fillets. She thought she would put the fish under the grill to cook, but she had one surprise visitor who arrived home with her husband. So the option was to cut the fish into several pieces. Life is all about experiencing and choosing the best course of action. She followed the recipe below and it came out as a fantastic dish - combining the flavour of the fish, the spices and white wine. She is French.

Ingredients - SERVES 2-3

Fresh trout (500-700 gm)
4 medium size potatoes
Natural yogurt
1/2 tsp salt
l onion
2 tomatoes
1/4 cauliflower
25 gm garlic
4 tsp tumeric powder
1 tsp panch phorong (five spice)
4 green chilis
Half glass white wine (optional)
Hot water

Direction

Marinade the trout (cut in medium size pieces) in yogurt, turmeric, salt for half an hour. Fry the fish in shallow oil, turning occasionally.

Fry the chopped onion and tomatoes, potatoes cut in slices, and cauliflower cut into small pieces - along with chopped garlic, panch phorong, sliced green chilis, and turmeric powder, for 5 minutes.

Add the fish and fry gently with white wine for about 2 minutes

Add half a cup of hot water and simmer for 10 minutes till the gravy is thick

SERVE WITH RICE DISH, FLAT BREAD WRAP OR LOOCHI

If you can't get Hilsa, a good alternative is Herring

Hilsa (Elish) Festival
A Bone to Pick!

Hilsa is the most sought after fish in India and Bangladesh, but it has thin bones. Hilsa Festival is a food fete when a variety of preparation of Hilsa is made. You buy the whole fish and slice into pieces across the width. The whole fish may weigh between 750 gm and 2kg. Larger the size, the tastier it is.

Hilsa Fry (Elish Maach Vaja)

Put the cut fish into a large container. Sprinkle turmeric power and salt (approx 6 tsp turmeric and 2 tsp salt per kg of fish). Pour mustard oil (250 ml per 1 kg) in a large frying pan enough for deep frying the fish. Once the oil is very hot, drop the pieces of fish into the pan and fry until crisp. Eat fried Hilsa as a starter, with salad.

Hilsa Vapa (Elisher Vapa)

Mix 100 gm posto with 50 gm sliced green chilies, 50 gm whole mustard seeds (for 1kg Hilsa fish), and use a grinder/mixer to make it into a paste. Cut another 50 gm of green chilies into small pieces.

Add 25 ml mustard oil and sprinkle 2 tsp turmeric powder over fish in an oven-proof bowl. Mix Hilsa pieces with the posto and mustard paste. Add the green chilies,1 tsp salt, and juice from one whole lemon. Place the bowl in the oven (covered in foil) or microwave. Cook for 150 minutes in oven at 150 degrees, or 10 minutes in a microwave.

Hilsa Pickle (Elisher Tok)

Deep fry Hilsa heads in the oil left on the frying pan and strain out. Break the heads into many pieces and mix with all broken pieces of fried Hilsa fish.

Boil 1 sliced Indian radish. In a separate pan fry 6 cut tomatoes with juice from two lemons, 1 boiled peeled green mango (or use mango chutney or mango jam), 1 tsp salt, the radish, and two cups hot water.

Boil for 5 mins and then add the fried Hilsa pieces. Cook for a further 10 mins. Adjust the water to make thick or thin gravy .

SERVE WITH PLAIN BOILED RICE AND SALAD. YOUR FESTIVAL IS COMPLETE

Hilsa Tel (Elish Tel)

The oil left in the frying pan can now be spooned over plain rice.

Liver Fever

The tastiest part of a bird or meat is the liver. A favourite liver dish in the west is liver and bacon, with sage. In India there are many dishes that can be made with liver. Liver can just be fried and cooked with spices to make it very tasty. However hybrid recipes of liver are more interesting. Two example are given below, for 300gm of liver:

Liver Indian Style

Ingredients - SERVES 2

500 gm lamb/chicken liver
100 gm onion
100 gm potatoes
2 tomatoes
4 tsp tumeric
2 tsp garam masala
50 gm garlic or paste
50 gm ginger or paste
1 tsp chili powder
1 tsp dhania powder
1 tsp cumin powder
1 tsp salt

Direction

Soak lambs/chicken liver in milk over night. Leave covered in a fridge.

Fry onion and potato cut into long slices, with turmeric, garam masala, chopped garlic or paste, chopped ginger or paste, chili powder, dhania powder, cumin powder, and salt. Fry together, then add chopped tomatoes. Add the liver, and fry until liver turns dark.

Pour over hot water and cook to your taste and thickness of gravy.

Liver & Bacon British Style

Ingredients - SERVES 2

300 gm lambs liver
4-6 rashers of streaky bacon
1 large onion
2 tomatoes
50 gm garlic
50 gm ginger
Tamari or 1 stock cube
Half level tsp pepper
4-6 leaves of sage
Salt to taste (salt in bacon)

SERVE WITH RICE DISH, FLAT BREAD
WRAP OR LOOCHI

Direction

Dip liver into plain flour and fry each side until flour absorbed. Place to one side. Fry bacon and onion, garlic and ginger together in same pan until onions sweat down. Add with the liver into a casserole dish. Then add a large cup of hot water, sage, pepper, tomatoes, tamari or stock cube, to flavour. Place in oven with lid on for about one hour. Start oven hot at 200 degrees and turn down to 180 after 15 minutes. Towards the end check the dish and add extra water, if too dry.

SERVE WITH THINLY FRIED ONION SPRINKLED OVER THE TOP, KASA MANGSO AND, MOST IMPORTANTLY, RAITA - MADE UP OF NATURAL YOGURT (CURD) AND SLICED CUCUMBER. ADD SALT TO TASTE.

Quick Biryani
(not so quick!) SERVES 6

Biryani is a majestic dish. Hence, cumbersome to cook. In most restaurants it takes almost 3 hours to cook biryani, and normally the biryanis served are very rich and spicy in nature. Here is a simplified and healthy biryani recipe for you to try cooking at home for Chicken, Mutton or Lamb. Alternatively use your choice of vegetables:

1. Marinate Chicken / Mutton / Lamb...*Marinate for about 2 hours:*
1 kg meat cut in large pieces (say, 8 pieces in 1 kilogram of meat) • 100 gm chopped garlic
6 tsp turmeric • 2 tsp chili powder • I whole lemon juice • 2 tsp salt • 8 tsp cooking oil

2. Fry Chicken / Mutton / Lamb
200 gm of peeled potatoes cut to 3⁄4 inch
4 bay leaves • 8 tsp ginger paste
8 tsp briyani mix/massala powder
100 gm cooking oil or 50 gm butter
1 glass red wine (optional)
Fry meat from stage 1. for approx 15 mins, with all of the above. Add wine during frying to soften the meat and give flavour. The cooked dish should be dry.

3. Basmati Rice Preparation
1 kg basmati rice
6 bay leaves • 2 tsp sugar
2 tsp cardamom pods • 1 tsp salt
6-8 tsp cooking oil
2 cinnamon sticks • 2 tsp cloves
1/4 litre water
Boil all of the above together for 5 minutes to half cook the rice. Drain water making each rice grain separate. Let it cool.

4. Cook on Electric Hob, Induction Cooker, Microwave, or Boiling Water
Pour 2 tsp cooking oil in an air-tight pot that can be placed on heat. Arrange one layer of half-cooked rice from Stage 3, with bay leaves. Then add a layer of meat from Stage 2. Lay a second layer of rice, then a second layer of meat. Try to make 3 layers. Cover the pot with lid and place on a high indirect heat such as induction hob, electric oven, or microwave. In the case of gas hobs, put the biryani pot inside a larger pot of boiling water and place on the hob - ensuring that the water doesn't get inside to the biryani mix. Boil for 15 -20 minutes until the rice and meat are cooked. With microwave you may only need 10 -15 minutes.

Fry 6 boiled eggs separately in turmeric and oil for 2 minutes and then add to the biryani in the final 10 minutes of cooking. Sprinkle over 2 tsp garam masala and 6 tsp melted butter. Rest for half an hour - air tight.

Fried Rice
Prawn / Egg / Chicken

Chinese takeaway is the theme nowadays. To make Chinese food tastier, some people add mono sodium glutamate (MSG). This is very harmful to the stomach. Although there are set limits, who follows the limits when it comes to taste? A few years ago there was a drive in India to avoid MSG, above a certain level. But the cooks in my restaurant wouldn't follow the limits, hence we banned it completely. The cooks went on strike but, with the help of the internet, we found alternate recipes. We then displayed posters in the restaurant informing customers of the risks of MSG, and that we do not use it in our cooking. Soon it became the norm to cook food without it. New tastes developed.

Ingredients - SERVES 4

500 gm basmati rice
100 gm white onion
100 gm garlic
50 gm broccoli florets
Half a cauliflower
2 capsicums
10 large mushrooms
2 large carrots
100 gm shrimps
2 eggs
100 gm chicken
100 gm butter
100 ml cooking oil
2 bay leaves
2 small cinamon sticks
10 cardamom pods
6 cloves
2 tsp salt

Note: you may also cook using prawn, chicken and egg separately.

SERVE WITH ANY VEGETABLE OR NON-VEG SIDE DISH, OR SALAD

Direction

Boil rice (half-cooked) and drain to make every rice separate - not pasty.

Fry chopped garlic and onion, florets of broccoli and cauliflower, sliced carrot, sliced capsicum, sliced mushroom, with salt, and a little sugar (half tps).

Boil shrimps/chicken for 5 minutes or use pre-cooked ingredients.

Fry the shrimps and sliced chicken in a separate frying pan for 5 minutes. Break two eggs into the same pan and stir with a fork for two minutes, to make the egg disintegrate.

Add rice to the fried vegetables and add butter and white oil. Fry for 5 minutes, then add the prawn, chicken and egg mixture, and fry for a further 5 minutes, with bay leaves, cinnamon sticks, cardamom, and cloves. When finished, place butter on top and ground black pepper. Cover for half an hour.

Child's Play
Mughlai Paratha

In September 2020, whilst the lockdown was almost over in India, there was a distinct fear in the air about infection with Covid 19, and social distancing was expected to be maintained. One such village family had an additional problem - the housewife having a serious illness (not Covid related). Their nine year-old son was trying to best help his mother, between his on-line study sessions, and assisting his mother in the home. He decided to make a Moughlai Parata as a variety, to make his mother smile. This is the story behind this dish. To make a proper Moughlai Parata precision is required. It is not a 'child's play' but a nine year-old boy making history by cooking simplified Moughlai Parata, as follows:

Ingredients - SERVES 2

2 potatoes
2 eggs
2 cups plain flour or ready-made wraps
1 medium onion
4 tsp garlic paste
6 green chilies
2 tsp sugar
2 tsp garam masala powder
4 tsp white oil
1 tsp chili powder
1 cup water
100 ml cooking oil

This is Child's Play Moughlai that every mother likes their son or daughter to make. Give your child the pleasure of cooking for you, to make them smile!

SERVE WITH ANY EGG SIDE DISH

Direction

Potatoes and eggs should be boiled first. Then fry with chopped onion and garlic for 5-10 minutes.

In a separate bowl, mix flour with sugar, salt, chili powder, sliced green chilies, garam masala and water to make it into a dough. Cut into 6 equal balls. Then roll the dough balls flat and thin - like chapattis.

Place a spoonful of the potato and egg mix at the center of one chapatti and make four folds from each of the four sides, to cover the mixture - making a square pouch. Put oil into a frying pan and spread one cracked egg. Cook lightly then put one folded chapatti onto the egg with the folded side down. Fry for 2-3 minutes, then turn over. Repeat until semi-brown and the dough is cooked

Please note: the folded side of the wrap will be fried with the egg. The other side will not always be covered by egg too.

Mexican Style Pork & Beans

This is an Englishman's recipe after getting exhausted of hearing about the preparation of this recipe book - in which his entire family of Indian origin is contributing. Here he has given his best - taking us to Mexico.

Ingredients - SERVES 2

500 gm diced pork belly
1 large onion
5-6 cloves
8 tsp garlic paste
200 gms beans (butter, kidney, haricot, cannelini, flageolet, bariotti, lima, pinto or a mix)
7 medium size tomatoes
2 capsicums
2 tsp chili powder
2 tsp prapika
4 tsp cumin seeds
6 green chilies
100 ml cooking oil
1 pint of stock
1 tsp salt

Direction

Prepare beans
Soak beans in water for a couple of hours. Fry cumin seeds in oil until sizzling, then add 1 chopped tomato, chili and paprika, and beans. Cover with water.

Cook in pressure cooker for 15 minutes and add beans to the rest of the dish. Prepare stock using pork or veg stock cubes, to taste.

Cook Pork Belly
In a large pan with lid, fry cumin seeds, chopped onion, chopped garlic, paprika, and chili, until sizzling. Add diced pork belly, chopped capsicums and tomatoes, salt, pepper, and cooked beans.

Simmer for 15-20 minutes until liquid is reduced, and all ingredients are soft and tender.

SERVE WITH RICE, FLAT BREAD OR WRAP

Chippy Turkey

Variety is the spice of life, and it was proved once again when my friend said she wanted us to make a special dish for friends - who had already tasted my other dishes, with full enjoyment. Reputation for a chef is the key, and to cook a new dish is a challenge!

Trev, the local Chipping Norton butcher, could not get me a partridge but offered left over turkey from Christmas. Then, surprise, surprise, the only veggie's left in the local shop (after the holiday) were spinach, leek, tomato and potatoes. We experimented as:

Ingredients - SERVES 4

500 gm diced turkey
25 gm garlic
25 gm ginger
50ml cooking oil
4 tsp tumeric
1 tsp chili powder
1 tsp salt
6 tsp brandy (optional)
100gm potatoes
1 leek
1 large onion
3 green chilis
3 medium tomatoes
2 tsp hot curry powder
2 tsp garam massala
1/2 litre water
100gm spinach

Direction

Fry turkey with onions, garlic and ginger in white oil for 10 minutes. Add tumeric, chili powder, salt and fry for a further 5 mintes. Pour in brandy as an optional extra, for flavour.

Add small cut potato, the leek cut as rings, 3 green chili's cut lengthways, and chopped tomatoes. Also add hot curry powder and garam massala, and fry for 25 minutes.

Then pour over 1/2 litre of hot water and simmer for 15 minutes.

During the last 5 minutes, sprinkle 100gm of chopped spinach over the top to sweat down.

SERVE WITH MASH POTATOES MIXED WITH CHOPPED ONION AND BUTTER, BOILED RICE OR WRAP

Grandma's 101st Birthday...

It was in a remote village, 300 km from Kolkata - my birth place - and it was my grandmother's 101st birthday.

At 2 pm, on a Sunday, we (the large family) all of a sudden, decided that we would like to have a birthday party for Grandma and invite the whole village of 60 families, that same evening.

A team was sent out to go house-to-house with invitations, and I with another team went into the nearest town, 7 km away, to buy groceries, vegetables and meat. A third team agreed to put up canopies and clear the area.

Shopping was done for some 150 people, and utensils hired.

Preparation

Preparation for cooking started at 6 pm, but it took longer than we had thought. Everybody was still very excited, then the nervousness started to grow. The clay oven was ready but there was nothing ready to cook until 7.30pm. We finally put the meat on one oven, and rice on top of another.

Initial problems

The colour wasn't developing in the 20 kg of meat, so we put 1 cup of sugar during the frying to give a nice colour. We then added 4 kg of fried onions, 1 kg of garlic, and 10 kg of potatoes and stirred with spices. We added hot water, but the meat was still tough after much cooking!

Guests had already arrived. My sister suggested that we serve them the thin gravy of the meat curry as soup. Which we did and it was very welcome as a starter.

...Clay Oven Cooking

My cousin said that the meat tasted "too hot", so we added sugar. Somebody later said "too sweet now", so we added more chili. It went into a number of iterations.

The meat was still tough, so we added a chopped green papaya and that helped tenderise.

Finally, the meat curry was ready, lentils were ready, and also the rice.

Real Problem

Everybody sat down and dinner was served. The food was simply marvellous.

But my grandmother noticed something unnatural and she asked me "Why are the people laughing so much? I have never seen them so jolly before".

In another corner, I found my sister and a friend of mine were fighting over a large cooking trough - as to who should wash it! My sister said she cooked the lentil, therefore she has the right to wash. Whereas, my friend said he helped her put the trough on the clay oven, so he had the right! After much fun and laughter the pot got cleaned!

The fact of the matter was - the combination of sugar and chili developed a 'wine effect' and everbody was intoxicated, but in a nice way! The party ended at midnight. Everyone went home happy!

Moral of the Story:

Cooking with LOVE for grandmother matters

Snowy Darjeeling...

Two young boys went to climb over the Himalayas on push bikes with their parents following in a 4x4, in freezing January. Somehow we all reached Darjeeling and the boys collapsed, so tired. More so were the parents and family (we were eight people altogether). We stayed for a week in Darjeeling, as our base camp, before moving on to Nepal and Sikkim. Almost all the hotels and restaurants were shut but we managed to get a hotel with one large hall to accomodate all of us. We then went to a local supermarket and bought a Rice Cooker - the only option left to survive for next 4 days.
It was a struggle in sub-zero Darjeeling!

Preparation

Ingredients we bought:

Rice, lentils/dal, salt , butter, bread, eggs, cauliflower, onions, turmeric, chili powder, green chilies, sugar, tea and coffee. They were all bought from a small local shop - with a store keeper who was too intoxicated to count the money!

What did we cook and how:

My brother-in-law was an accountant but he could always do better as an engineer, so he was in put in charge of making sure the rice cooker worked. The young boys had hot blood; hence they were never asked to do the washing up in semi-warm water.

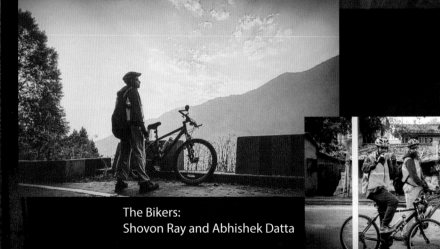

The Bikers:
Shovon Ray and Abhishek Datta

...Lonely Rice Cooker

Khichuri with Butter

We warmed water in the rice cooker. Then we added rice , lentil, chopped onions, garlic, potatoes, turmeric, chili powder, and salt, cooked it for an hour or so and then dropped in eggs with more water. This dish took almost three hours to cook . Hungry cyclists and family found it welcoming and delicious.

Hot Chicken Curry and Rice

Turmeric and chili powder was mixed in hot water to make a paste, which was used to marinate the cut chicken - for two hours. Potatoes and onions were then boiled in the rice cooker. Next we cooked the marinated chicken in the rice cooker for one hour or so and then half the boiled potatoes and onions were added. Then we cooked rice. The whole meal took us some three hours, or so. Delicious!

Egg Curry and Rice / Bread

This was much simpler to cook but the bread was cold. We had to cook rice but by that time that was finished, the egg curry was cold, so we had to boil it again! Still delicious.

Did we go on to Nepal and Sikkim? Wait for my next book!

Morale of the story:

Cooking for family with CARE matters

Bongo Santans (Bengalees)

Microwave

People from Kolkata are commonly known as "Bongo Santan", myself being one. We find our own food, wherever we go. But the Hamburg Rotary Convention was an exception. Ten of us were there for a week or so. Bongo Sontans normally get excited too soon, then it subsides. Same happened here in Hamburg, everyone was excited about German food, to begin with.

Since I visited Europe so many times I wanted to stick to my home-cooked style of food, but not with 'Indian Restaurant' richness. I asked the hotel manager for a microwave so that I could prepare my own food, in my own suite. He took some persauding!

Soon, I heard all my mates knocking on my door asking to share my food. Wine is cheaper than water in Germany and I was cooking with wine. That was the main attraction. The Hamburg Convention became 'fun and games' cooking for 10 people, using a single microwave oven!

Ingredients
Rice, lentils, potatoes, peas, mash potato powder, onions, eggs, cooked turkey, carrots, skinless sausages, courgettes, runner beans, turmeric paste, garlic paste, chili sauce, salt, pepper, margarine/butter,

...and plenty of wine!

...at Rotary Convention

Direction

Peas Rice

Put 200 gm rice, 50 gm peas, 2 cut carrots s and half a litre of water in a micro oven cooking box and cook for 10 minutes. It was perfect.

Turkey Curry

Mix 400 gm of turkey pieces with 6 tsp turmeric, 6 tsp chili sauce, 100 gm chopped onion, 1 chopped courgette, 4 tsp garlic paste, 2 tsp salt, 6 tsp margarine, 3 glasses red wine with half a cup of water in a micro oven cooking pot. Cook for 10-15 minutes. It was perfect.

Mash Sausages

Cut 20 cooked sausages into very small pieces and mixed with 100 gm mash potato powder, 2 tsp turmeric, 6 tsp chili sauce, 100 gm green peas and 6 tsp margarine. Mix well, then add 2 glasses red wine with a sprinkle of water and 1 tsp salt in a micro oven cooking pot. Cook for 10 minutes. It was perfect.

Egg Curry ... It was not perfect!

We were boiling 10 eggs in the microwave oven and it exploded!!! ...making the power supply go off on the entire floor! It was because **we didn't add salt when boiling the eggs (important tip!).**

Anyway, after cleaning up the room in a panic, we corrected our cooking method and put boiled potatoes together with boiled eggs, along with 4 tsp turmeric, 4 tsp garlic, 2 tsp chili sauce, 2 glasses of wine and a cup of water into pot. We cooked for 10 minutes.

The food was far from being perfect, but my friends watched me cook while discussing Rotary, This raised their appetite. After that they enjoyed my cooking for a futher 5 days!

Moral of the Story:

Cooking for friends with FUN matters

Bengali Rossogolla

Ingredients - 20 PIECES

1 cup semolina
4 cups milk
1 cup white sugar
4 tsp rose water (optional)
2 tsp ghee/butter
1 1⁄2 cup water

SERVE AS AN INDEPENDENT
SWEET DISH

Direction

Mix semolina with milk and sugar (half a cup) and boil. Stir slowly to make it thick. Continue on medium heat until it becomes a dough. Let it cool down.

Mix half a cup of sugar with 1 1⁄2 cups of water. Add cardamom (elichi) and boil on low flame to make into a syrup.

Make 20 dough balls (1/2 to 1 inch in diameter) from the semolina/milk dough, (made as above), with a touch of ghee or butter, to help each ball hold together.

Drop the dough balls into the syrup and boil on low flame for 15 -20 minutes. Then rest for 1 hour in air-tight container.

OVER COOKING: If you boil Rossogolla too long the syrup dries, caramalises, and turns into Danadar...also delicious!

African Banana Fritter

Ingredients - SERVES 2

6 bananas
4 tsp turmeric powder
Cooking oil

Direction

Peel 6 bananas and chop each into 3-4 pieces. Sprinkle turmeric powder all round the banana pieces, and shallow fry in oil until both sides are browned and caramilised. Leave to cool for one hour.

SERVE WITH ICE CREAM
OR FRESH CREAM

Bedtime Noodles for tired mother

Gather together 500 gms pasta or noodles, 1 capsicum, chopped spring onion, mushrooms, chopped carrot, peas, garlic paste, vegetable oil. (You can add 200 gm cream cheese, other vegetables, and use left overs from your kitchen too).

Make a simple sauce:
Heat oil and add garlic paste. Add mushrooms with the other ingredients and sauté. Add chopped bacon/ham for flavour, if you like.

Boil pasta in water with salt separately.

Then add few spoonfuls of salt water from the pasta, along with the cream cheese, and cook on low heat for 15 minutes.

Drain pasta and mix into the sauce.

Garnish with Cheddar or Parmesan cheese, and serve.

Good Night

Master Class

"*The Masterclass with Saumen was just inspiring. His clear instructions and explanations of how to cook these onion bhajis (right) was really informative and so much fun! The fact that I could actually repeat the process easily at home in my own kitchen is testament to this. You can feel his joy for cooking and most definitely taste it in his food!*

I'm now confident in rustling up these delicious onion bhajis whenever the mood takes me. I do truly love eating them!"

Carol Love, Gloucestershire, UK

"*The Master Class led by Saumen (avove) was well prepared. His passion, creativity, and enthusiasm for sharing his favourite dishes, shone through. He kept us entertained throughout with stories, some traditional and some contemporary, relating to the dishes we prepared.*"
Nicola Menage, Oxfordshire, UK

•••••

"*It was a memorable evening sampling Saumen's cuisine, and I am sure your recipe book would be helpful to reproduce the dishes. I really enjoyed the banana fritters, and asked Saumen how they were done - I cannot have properly understood his method as my first attempt was a very limited success, so there is another reason for your book being helpful!*"
Jonathan Guido, Oxfordshire, UK

"At first, I was fearful of the amount of spices and chili Saumen is suggesting here. However, during cooking, the ingredients blend together with the meat or fish and vegetables, absorbing the richness to produce a delicious dish. I now understand the balance of sweet and spicy, and enjoy the chutney (left) which compliments the heat of the spice. I have been cooking Saumen's recipes for the past year, and feel good...healthier."

Gill de Warren, Oxfordshire, UK

• • • • •

"This is really wonderful, like love and cooking. This is a new concept both in the West and in the East. Congratulations for your Humility and self deprecation they are the traits of the greater souls.

I love what I see on the front cover and pages two and three. Especially because, you have included three generations of your family value. People will separate your book out of hundreds of books on the book sellers' shelves. As a writer-critique, I have got to be Honest and Constructive in my critique. I have no doubt, the public will love it, as I have. I wish you very best of luck and joy with your book. With love and best wishes."

Arun and Ratna Debnath Harrow, London, UK

Dear Saumen,

It is truly a very motivating information that, you have written two books on two diverse subjects during your home stay in London, due to a pandemic. I think you have used your time in the most productive manner, using the window of opportunity provided by the COVID-19 virus and, of course, it is in sync with the current theme of Rotary.

Having gone through a few pages, I find it is fascinating and press worthy. I wish you all the best towards the success of your books in India, and abroad.
Thanking you,
Yours-in-Rotary,

PDG Anirudha Roychowdhury (D-3291), Kolkata, India

RPIC - Zone 6
DRFC (2019 - 22)
Assistant Rotary Coordinator for Zone - IV (2010 - 2013)
Assistant Rotary Public Image Coordinator (2013 - 2015)
Assistant Rotary Regional Foundation Coordinators (2016 - 2017)
Secretary - Rotary India Literacy Mission
District COL Representative 2013

FAQ's
Tips & Tricks

Too sweet
Add chili and salt, and cook for an extra 5 minutes.

Feeling depressed in cooking
Put the radio on for your favourite music. Cook with Love in your heart.

Gravy/sauce too thin
Break eggs and stir in. Cook as normal.

Food doesn't look too colourful
Fry 1 tsp of sugar with 3 tsp of oil for 2 minutes and then pour over the cooked food. Fry or boil for 5 minutes.

Too spicy or rich
Pour in boiling water and salt, and stir. Leave until the spices and oil start to separate and float. Drain off the water mixed with spice and oil.

Too salty
Add an appropriate quantity of lemon and sugar and fry or boil for 5 minutes.

Some vegetable are still not soft
Add half tsp baking powder and cook as normal.

Too much turmeric
Half burn/scorch 2 or 3 bay leaves on a flame. Dip the burnt bay leaf in the cooked food and continue cooking for 5 minutes.

Meat still not tender
Add green papaya and cook normally.

Too much chili
Add lemon/vinegar/tomato with a little sugar and cook for 5 minutes.

Food catches on bottom of the pan
Empty the contents into a fresh pan, add vinegar or lemon to help remove any burnt taste, and boil as appropriate.

NOTES